Dedicated to

Mr. Virgil H. Swift, Jr.

April 13, 1947–August 25, 2009

Mr. Swift, a member of the Wichita Tribe, worked to preserve the language and customs of his people; he urged everyone to accept all cultures, and treat others with compassion and respect. His heart was full of kindness, love, and generosity for his fellow man.

Acknowledgments

Virginia Wulfkuhle and Robert J. Hoard, of the Kansas State Historical Society, Topeka, Kansas, for graciously providing images of grass houses and artifacts.

Special thanks to Marlin F. Hawley, Wisconsin Historical Society, for his advice and assistance.

Mike Rooney adjusted various images and permitted the use of his award-winning photography.

Contents

Foreword

The Wichita Indians, People of the Grass House by Susan A. Holland is a brief, non-technical introduction to an important central and southern Plains tribe. Illustrated with a number of stunning, full-color pictures by Mike Rooney, *The Wichita Indians* quickly reviews the archaeology and ethnography of the Wichita, a powerful Native American confederation with village clusters in Rice and McPherson counties above the Great Bend of the Arkansas River, Marion County on the Cottonwood River, Butler and Cowley counties on the Walnut River, and in Wilson County on the Verdigris River. Although Susan's remarks generally cover all of the peoples of the confederation, they derive from her experiences as the director of Kansas State Historical Society's (KSHS) field archaeology laboratory, based in Arkansas City, Kansas, in the mid-1990s. I directed the overall project for several years.

At the time, the KSHS was involved in a multi-year project to salvage archaeological materials in advance of highway and levee construction. The sites there, located on the eastern edge of Arkansas City, had been known since the 1870s and were the subject of important investigations in 1940 by Dr. Waldo R. Wedel, of the U.S. National Museum, Smithsonian Institution. The excavations of the mid-1990s were far larger than Wedel's small crew could ever have dreamed of, as the twin construction projects cut a wide swathe north-south and east-west across the floor of the Walnut River valley. The excavations, as Susan notes, revealed the remains of hundreds of storage pits, many filled to various degrees with trash or with only a few objects, such as pots or other tools, smaller pits, often of unknown use, and traces of buildings. Susan focuses on the distinctive beehive, grass houses, of the Wichita, but finding the remains of these buildings, which once must have dotted the valley floor in the hundreds, proved difficult. The reason is not so hard to understand, as the fertile valley floor came under the plow beginning in the 1870s. The posts supporting structures, like houses, work platforms, or arbors (for shade), were set shallowly into the ground and few post patterns survived cultivation.

The archaeological sites in the valley there beside Arkansas City seem to have been part of a large village—aptly called the Great Settlement or now sometimes the Lower Walnut Settlement—visited by the Spanish in 1601. Documents describe neighborhoods of houses and other buildings set apart by gardens. Estimates of the population varied wildly, but modern scholars think this sprawling village complex may have been home to as many as 10,000 men, women and children. As Susan so well describes it, broad expanse of the valley and the surrounding hills supplied land for fields, fish, waterfowl, and game, such as deer, elk, and bison. Women made pottery and flintknappers quarried stone from the southern Flint Hills to make arrow points, knives, and scrapers. Animal bone was crafted into needles, awls, scrapers, and even hoes and other digging implements.

It is Susan's fondest hope, and mine as well, that this volume will serve not as an introduction to the archaeology of the Lower Walnut Settlement, but will pique the interest of readers to explore the rich history and ethnography of the Wichita peoples. To that end, she has included a brief list of further books and papers to explore.

Marlin F. Hawley

Marlin F. Hawley was Project Director on the Arkansas City, Kansas, project for the Kansas State Historical Society from 1991 to 1997. He co-authored two chapters in the final report and has numerous other publications associated to Kansas.

Introduction

The American Indians, including the Wichita, shared the prairie of the Great Plains, in the central United States, with a large variety of fauna and flora. Everything they needed for survival was present.

Prior to the start of European agriculture practices in the 1800s, the prairie extended from the Rocky Mountains east to the Mississippi River, and from Texas north to Canada. At present, only 4% of that prairie still exists. The main groundcover was big bluestem grass which could grow up to 12 feet high.

The Wichita Indians cut and bundled this tall prairie grass to use in the construction of their unique, beehive-shaped grass houses. This grass was the main food for millions of American Bison and elk which roamed the area, and provided cover, nesting, and seed, for the large variety of song and game birds that resided there. Over

800 different species of wildflowers and plants grew in this rich area. River and wetland ecosystems contained fish, mollusks, turtles, beaver, raccoons, and other mammals. The waterways also attracted hundreds of migrating waterfowl every year.

The Flint Hills, located in the eastern half of Kansas, were formed over 250 million years ago when flint, or chert-bearing limestone, was deposited by shallow inland seas. The flint, located either on or close to the surface, was prized by the Wichita for use in making their tools, weapons, and projectile points. It also made 19th century farming practices impossible, thus helping to preserve the 4% of the original prairie we now have.

Today, driving across the gently rolling prairie of the Flint Hills, grazing livestock can be seen scattered over the landscape. The carpet of green prairie grass still provides excellent grazing, and this, along with fire, permits few trees from growing in the area. Prairie fires, possibly caused by lightning when the Wichita lived here, cleared dead vegetation, returning essential nutrients to the soil. The American Indians realized the importance of fire and, possibly, set fires themselves if Mother Nature failed. Present day ranchers set fire to the dead ground cover in the early spring, and driving through the area, you may spot fires, or plumes of smoke, and see the blackened areas. Once burned, new green plant life sprouts almost immediately.

The origins and migrations of the Wichita Indians are somewhat unclear. Coronado encountered bands of Wichita speaking people north of the Great Bend of the Arkansas River, in central Kansas, around 1541. In approximately 1601, Juan de Onate visited, what he termed, "the Great Settlement," consisting of homes, structures, and gardens, spread over a couple square miles, in the Lower Walnut River area of southern Kansas. After residing in the central plains, various bands migrated southward into modern Oklahoma and northern Texas around 1690-1791. The city of Wichita, Kansas, and Wichita Mountains are named after them.

People of the Grass House

The Wichita Indians called themselves Kitkit'sh, or Kidikides, which means "raccoon-eyed." The name came from one of their old legends about a man who transformed himself into an animal called "Dog-of-a-Child" and had

Raccoon showing black mask around its eyes

a child with a raccoon. In ancient times, the Wichita were said to be able to transform into an animal and then back into a human. The Wichita men tattooed dark circles around their eyes to resemble the natural black mask on a raccoon, thus giving them the name. This differentiated them from their close relatives, the Pawnee and Caddo, who also tattooed their bodies but not heavily around their eyes.

The Wichita lived on the Great Plains, in the present states of Kansas, Oklahoma, and Texas. A distinctive feature of their culture was the beehive-shaped grass houses they lived in. These large homes were constructed of wood poles covered with bundles of long prairie grass.

Wichita grass houses and gardens

These large, permanent structures could last up to fourteen seasons before they needed to be replaced. Wichita villages, located on bench areas, were near rivers and waterways with their

gardens planted in lower areas to receive moisture and rich silt during high water. The crops
included maize (corn), squash, pumpkins, sunflowers, and tobacco. Wild plants growing in the
area provided a variety of fruit, including plums,
grapes, and blackberries. Nuts and seeds were
harvested from walnut, hickory, and oak trees.

The women were responsible for tending the
gardens and gathering food. The Wichita men
were hunters, having a large resource of birds,
fish, and game animals to choose from.

The river area provided a variety of fish, turtles, and mussels. Fish included: catfish, gar,
drum, crappie, and bluegill. Turtles, both hard
and soft shelled, had seven different kinds of
delicious meat and were good sources of protein.
Turtle shells were made into ornaments and rat-
tles, and were used as cutting and scraping tools.

The confluence of the Arkansas River and
Lower Walnut River, in south-central Kansas,
was one homeland of the Wichita. This is still one
of the most inundated bird migration flyways in
North America. Annual bird migrations, taking
place in the spring and fall, includes hundreds of
various species whose flight path stretches from
Canada to southeast Texas.

Birds of varying sizes migrate annually. Some
of the larger species are Canada and Snow Geese,
Sandhill Cranes, swans, and pelicans. Smaller

Hundreds of migrating birds at Kansas wetlands

migratory birds include robins, sparrows, hummingbirds, and red-winged blackbirds.

One bird, the wild turkey, was a permanent resident, providing food and feathers year-around. Turkeys were kept in captivity by American Indians for centuries and were a source of food, eggs, and feathers. Their tail feathers were used

Wild turkey

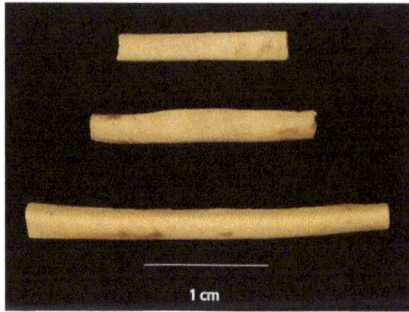

Bone beads

in dances and ceremonies, on prayersticks, fans, and for fletching on arrow shafts. The hollow leg bones of the turkey, and other large birds, were made into flutes, beads, and other items.

Wood ducks also migrated through the area. The male is one of the most colorful in North America with multi-colored dazzling feathers and red eyes. Wood ducks have sharp claws, giving them the unique ability to perch and nest in tree cavities. Their main food consists of seeds,

Male wood duck

acorns, berries, and insects. No doubt, their eye-catching feathers were collected and used.

Flickers, which are large woodpeckers, had their feathers utilized as fletching on arrows, like those of the turkey. The flicker, along with other woodpeckers and a number of song birds, was also a year-around resident. Bald eagles, vultures, falcons, various hawks, and owls also lived on the Great Plains.

Blue heron

Large wading birds hunt near banks and in shallow water. The graceful blue heron, holding its long neck in an S-shape, remains motion-less for long periods of time while it scans the area for prey. While standing in the water and spotting food, they can stike with lightning-fast precision, stretching out their neck, and impaling their target with a dagger-like, thick bill. The blue heron's food includes fish and, an ocassional gopher.

Bull elk

The water also attracks large game animal like deer, pronghorn, elk (or wapiti), and bison. These animals were an excellent source of meat for the Wichita. A bull, or male elk, could weight up to 1100 pounds and provide around 800 pounds of meat. The antlers, reaching four feet above its head, were shed every March and regrown by May, and could be made into tools. The male elk is the only North American animal that has ivories, also called whistle teeth. These two, upper, ivory teeth were collected by the Indians and used to decorate their clothing. Tanned skins from the elk, deer, and bison were made into clothing, mocassins, robes, and blankets. Bone awls and needles were used for sewing garments, and sinew (tendon from the legs of deer, elk, and bison) was used for thread.

As the bison herds moved across the prairie, the Wichita would leave their villages to hunt them. They fabricated temporary homes (grass house remains have been found at hunting camp sites) or, possibly took teepees to live in, during extended hunts. Twelve to fourteen tanned bison hides were fashioned into a teepee. The hides, sewn together in a half circle, were wrapped outside long teepee poles; the two sides were held together with long wooden pins, and the bottom secured to the ground with wooden stakes, forming the circular structure.

Horses did not arrive in North America until the Spanish brought them around 1540. Possessions, like teepees, were transported on hunts by attaching a V-shaped drag frame, with cross-bars, to a large dog.

The bison was the most crucial animal to the American Indian. They utilized 100% of this huge

Bull bison that has been in a wallow

animal. It was their main source of meat, which was cut into thin strips and hung on racks to dry. Tanned hides, with the hair left on, were used for bedding, warm blankets, and robes. Various bones were made into tools; the sinew was used for sewing and made excellent bow strings. The horns, which both the male and female have, were shaped into drinking cups and spoons. The internal organs, such as the bladder and stomach, were used as containers. Skulls from the bulls, with horns and hair attached, were used in ceremonial dances. The dried manure was burned as fuel, producing a hot fire. Nothing was wasted.

Bison calves were light brown or reddish. The babies were often bedded down in grass by their mother to conceal them while the adults grazed. This kept the young calf safe from predators, like coyotes and wolves. More than one calf could be placed together with a female "standing guard" over them. If calves were in danger, adults would protect them by enclosing the young in a circle and facing outward toward the threat. Adult bison are very aggressive, threatening beasts capable of intimidating other animals.

Bison calf

While the American Bison was necessary to the livelihood of the Indians, it also played an important part in the ecology of the land. The bulls would make and use large depressions in the ground called wallows, which held rain and formed waterholes for other animals and birds.

These areas were produced when the bulls would tear up the soil with their heavy horns, rub their shoulders in the loose dirt, and roll back and forth on their backs while holding their legs straight up in the air. Hair from their heavy, shaggy coat would mix with the mud and water, creating a water-proof bottom seal. Along with cleaning themselves, the mud helped protect them from insects and bugs.

Wichita Women

L abor was generally divided, with the men making weapons and hunting and the women growing and harvesting the crops, of which corn was the most important. One of their ceremonies was the Green Corn Dance, held several times a year. This dance offered up prayers and gave thanks for the corn.

Also important was the Spring Planting Ceremony to Evening Star and Her Sacred Garden. In Wichita mythology, Evening Star had the power to bring the rain, and her garden represented all plant and animal life on earth. Bison hoes, borrowed from the Sacred Bundles, were used in this ceremony by women who made hoeing motions symbolic of working the soil. The following morning the fields were planted.

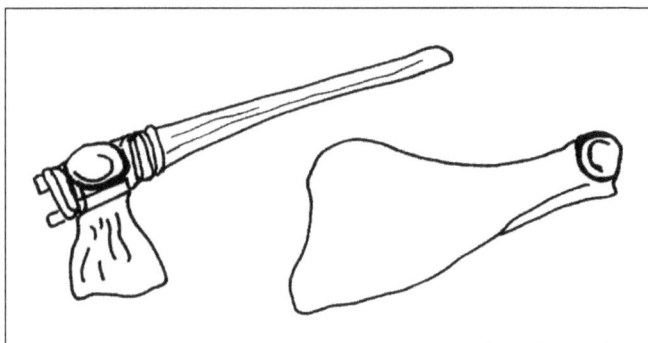

Bison scapula hoe and scapula bone

Bison scapula hoes, used in the gardens and fields, were made by attaching a wood handle to the socket end of the scapula, or shoulder blade bone. Bison scapulae are very large, heavy bones and the blade edge made an excellent agriculture tool. Along with tending crops, gathering natural resources, and fencing the gardens, the women also built the grass houses.

Stone ax

❶ Cutting posts

The early Native American Indians had no metal, so they fashioned tools, like axes, from stone. This stone, chert or flint, was gathered from the southern Flint Hills in present-day Cowley County, Kansas, and in Kay County, Oklahoma.

Axes were used by either holding them in a person's hand, or with an attached wood handle, similar to the ones on the scapula hoes.

A wood handle would have been fastened around the groove. The other end was tapered to a sharp edge to use for cutting and chopping.

The tibia, a very large, heavy, lower leg bone, had a handle attached at one end. The opposite end was beveled off into a spade-like shape and used to dig. The tool was held with the beveled end down and used like a modern spade or hoe.

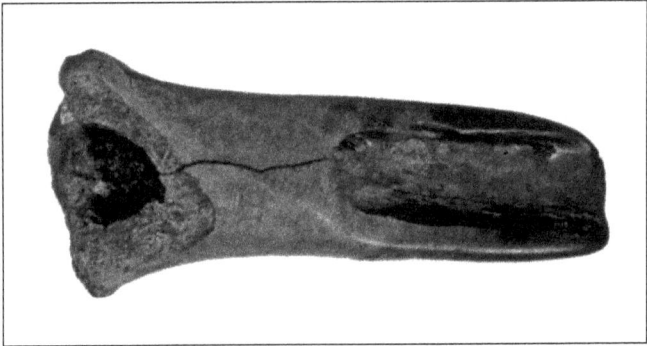

Bison tibia bone digging tool

The village leader first approved the construction of a new house. Everyone in the village helped to cut and gather the cedar poles, with the women doing the actual building. The poles, once cut, were stripped of bark to discourage insects and bugs from living in the wood. Bison bone tools were used to dig post holes and the four main upright poles were set first. The base of each pole had dirt pressed firmly around it to hold the post solidly upright in the ground, and sometimes wood and bone wedges were used to

❷ Large cedar post being placed in ground

hold the poles tight. Each post had a Y-shape at the top for horizontal poles to rest in.

Eight to sixteen upright cedar posts, depending on what size the house was to be, were set. Additional poles were then placed horizontally, with each end in the Y-notch of each upright post, completing a circle. These circles could have been up to 30 feet or more in diameter. Four longer, upright willow poles were then set in the ground outside the main cedar posts. These four smaller poles represented the four cardinal directions of north, south, east and west.

❸ Poles placed horizontally at top of cedar posts

The women, climbing the strong outer poles and standing on the upper horizontal beams, reached the upper area of the four long poles. These long poles, soaked in water to make them pliable, were pulled inward toward the center of the frame and tied to form a peak at the top of the house frame.

❹ Long, thin poles placed against frame

The tops of these four poles protruded from the top of the finished house representing the four sacred directions of the universe and earth. The very top, or peak, symbolized the Wichita Creator, the Great Spirit.

The tops of these four poles were purposely longer than the others. They were believed to be the main strength of the house, and were attributed to the Four Winds, or Sacred Directions, in Wichita mythology.

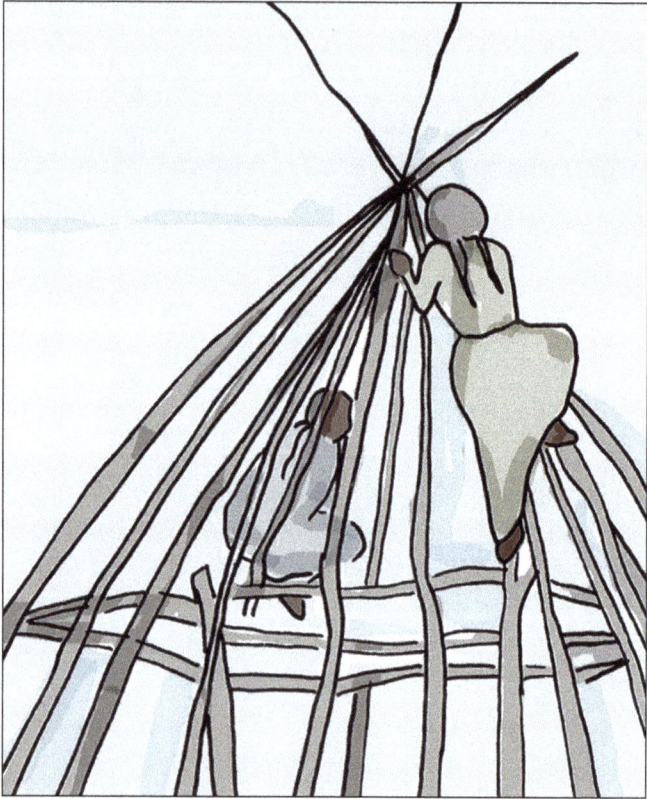

❺ Tops of poles are tied together

Smaller, upright willow poles were set into the ground so they were leaning on the frame, to which they were tied. This completed the upright frame.

Starting at the bottom, small, horizontal willow poles were attached to the uprights and tied with strips of bison leather. This was repeated on the upright structure, working upward until the top was reached. The skeletal framework of the

❻ Horizontal frame work

house was completed and ready for the bundles of the long prairie grass to be attached.

The first bundles were placed, standing vertically, at ground level with each successive layer overlapping the one below it. The grass was held in place by small, horizontal willow poles placed over it. Next, a very long bison bone needle (a grassing needle), was threaded with cordage, or string, and pushed through the grass. The cord was then wrapped around the small willow poles, attached to larger upright posts, and tied.

This process held the bundles of grass securely to the frame.

❼ Exterior of frame is covered with prairie grass

Grassing needles could be fashioned from either wood or bison rib bones. Ribs from an adult bison are thick bones, up to three feet long, and their gentle curve made them perfect items for this usage. A hole was drilled in one end with a stone drill, and the string, made from strips of

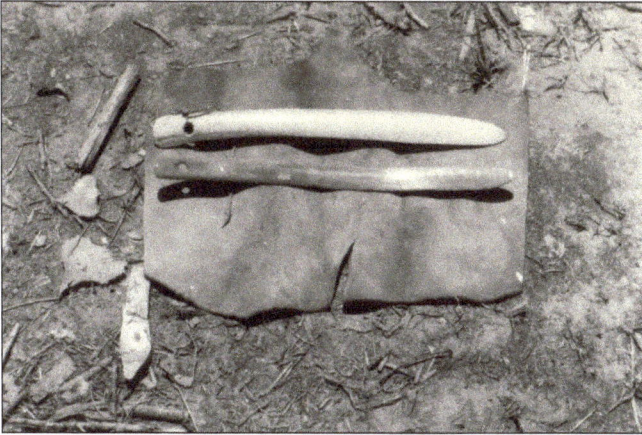

Grassing needles

the inner bark of elm trees, was threaded though the eye.

The process of adding the prairie grass was repeated, over-lapping the bundles of long grass around the frame. Working from the ground up repelled water and moisture, keeping the interior of the house dry. Two door areas were left open; one door faced east, so the morning sun could be seen, and the other door faced west, for the evening. Doors were also made of wood and prairie grass. They were not attached to the house, but leaned in place.

The fireplace, or hearth, was in the center of the interior so smoke could escape through the very top and the upper grass walls. Beds were located near the wall on pole frames, elevating them off the floor. Grass mattresses were covered by soft, tanned hides. In the winter, bison hides with the hair still attached, made warm blankets. The sleeping areas provided privacy by hanging tanned hides from horizontal poles of the inner frame. Various objects were also attached or hung from interior poles, keeping them off of the floor area to make more living space. Extended family lived in each house, so many people could have been present in a dwelling.

Completed grass house

These shared homes could last up to fourteen years if properly cared for. Early explorers observed villages consisting of large numbers of these grass houses, 80 to 120 buildings per village. One early Spanish report located a large village in the current area of Dodge City, in southwestern Kansas. This must have been a Wichita village as the Wichita Indians were the only Native Americans to construct houses using this technique.

Wood drying racks, for meat and vegetables, were located in areas between the houses. After

Grass houses and drying rack

drying, excess food was placed in large cache pits to preserve it.

These round cache, or storage, pits were completely concealed below ground level, and provided safety for food and stored items. The storage pit, which could be up to six feet deep, had a narrow top, or neck, and then belled out with a flat bottom. Once dug, the walls were lined with clay, and when dry, wood pegs placed in the walls held suspended bags of food and other items. Extra bone tools, tanned hides, and surplus food could be safely stockpiled out of sight. Because of their depth, the pits were cool, even in the summer, and kept stored items preserved. Access was gained by the use of a ladder, and the storage pits were only opened a few times a year to remove or add items. The tops, which were sealed and covered with soil, kept out rodents and water when it rained, and disguised their location. When the pits began to leak, or rodents dug into them, they were used as "dumps." These dumps preserved hundreds of items, thus providing a wealth of information for archeologists.

The Wichita stored food in leather bags, woven baskets, and pottery jars. The pottery was plainware, for daily use and cooking, and was not painted. Most vessels had small handles at the neck and a flat bottom.

Reconstructed pottery jar

A valuable record of American Indian agriculture that includes, among other things, the
construction, and cross-section drawing of a
cache pit, drawings of a drying rack, antler
rake and scapula hoe, is *Buffalo Bird Woman's
Garden.* The book was originally published as
*Agriculture of the Hidatsa Indians: An Indian
Interpretation* by Gilbert Livingston Wilson, Ph.
D., University of Minnesota, in 1917. Like the
Wichita, the Hidatsa culture depended on corn
and bison.

The Wichita Indians

The Wichita Indians were very resourceful and self-sufficient. They survived on the Great Plains, in the central United States, by taking advantage of the natural resources and wildlife they shared the region with.

Their villages consisted of unique, one-of-a-kind, grass houses constructed of wood poles and bundles of prairie grass. Their storage, or cache, pits were below ground level, and, when sealed, were completely hidden. These storage pits safeguarded extra food supplies and personal items.

Villages were located on bench areas near rivers where the lower garden plots received water and rich silt during high water. The gardens included maize (corn), squash, beans, sunflowers, and tobacco. Yearly agricultural ceremonies were performed at planting and harvesting times.

Rivers and wetlands attracted and contained a large number of mammals, fish, and birds, which supplemented their diet. The Wichita went on extended bison hunts to procure meat, hides, and bones, which were modified and used for tools. Millions of bison and elk once lived on the Great Plains, along with deer, pronghorn, and a variety other game animals.

Stone tools and projectile points were fashioned from naturally occurring chert deposited in the area around 250 million years ago. This material, from the Flint Hills, was highly prized by the American Indians.

Early Wichita villages were located in present-day Rice, McPherson, Cowley, Marion, and Wilson counties in Kansas.

The picture on the next page is courtesy of the National Archives at Fort Worth, Texas. It shows Wichita women, in their traditional clothing, building an old-time grass house. Everyone in the village helped cut and gather the poles, but women did the actual construction.

The upper portion of the structure shows the framework before the prairie grass was attached. At the very top, three of the four longest poles are shown. These four poles, which protruded from the top of every house, symbolized the four sacred directions of the universe and earth. The Wichita were the only Native Americans who built and lived in this unique style of grass house.

In the background, to the right, is a teepee which the Wichita used as a temporary home when they left the main village to go on extended bison hunts.

Wichita constructing grass house at
1903 St. Louis Exposition

Photo Credits

Page	Picture	Credit
i	grass house	Archeology Office, Kansas State Historical Society, Topeka, KS
iii	Mr. Virgil H. Swift	Marlin F Hawley, Wisconsin Historical Society
8	raccoon	Mike Rooney
9	Wichita grass houses	Archeology Office, KSHS, Topeka, KS
11	birds at wetlands	Mike Rooney
11	wild turkey	Mike Rooney
12	bone beads	*Archeological Investigations at Arkansas City, KS*, Contract Archeological Publication, No. 26, KSHS, Topeka, KS, Page 405
12	male wood duck	Mike Rooney

Page	Picture	Credit
13	blue heron	Mike Rooney
14	bull elk	Mike Rooney
16	bull bison	Mike Rooney
17	bison calf	Mike Rooney
20	bison scapula hoe	Susan A Holland
20	stone ax	* see below
21	cutting posts	* see below
22	tibia bone	* see below
23	posts placed in ground	* see below
24	horizontal posts	* see below
25	poles placed against frame	* see below
26	tops tied together	* see below
27	horizontal frame work	* see below
28	frame covered with grass	* see below
29	grassing needles	* see below
30	completed grass house	* see below
31	grass houses and drying racks	* see below

Page	Picture	Credit
33	reconstructed jar	*Archeological Investigations at Arkansas City, KS*, Contract Archeological Publication, No. 26, KSHS, Topeka, KS, Page 260
36	grass house at 1903 St. Louis Expo	National Archives, Ft. Worth, TX
44	rabbit effigy	Courtesy KSHS and KS Department of Transportation. Robert J. Hoard, editor *Archeological Investigations at Arkansas City Kansas* KSHS Contract Archeology Publication 26, KSHS, Topeka, KS
45	bone needle	
45	bone awls	
46	Washita points	
47	cache pit	

Front cover—Grass house at 1903 St. Louis, St. Louis Expo National Archives, Ft. Worth, TX

*Credits for illustrations on pages 21, 23-28, 30 and 31; and artifacts on pages 20, 22, and 29. Cali Letts, Virginia A. Wulfkuhle, Robert J. Hoard, 2012. STUDENT MAGAZINE *The Archaeology of Wichita Indian Shelter in Kansas*, Archaeology Popular Report Number 4, Kansas State Historical Society, Topeka.

Illustrations 21, 23-28, 30 and 31 of the grass house construction are on pages 10 and 11 in the STUDENT MAGAZINE; the stone ax pictured on page 20 is from page 14 in the STUDENT MAGAZINE, the tibia digging tool pictured on page 22 is from page 15 in the STUDENT MAGAZINE, and the grassing needles pictured on page 29 are from page 2 in the STUDENT MAGAZINE.

Epilogue

The inspiration for a book on the Wichita Indians is two conjoined highway archaeology projects in Arkansas City, Kansas, on which I was employed by the Kansas State Historical Society (KSHS). I had previously worked in the west, and southwestern U.S., where remains of prehistoric sites were generally highly visible. Since the Great Plains seemed to lack noticeable, above ground, features, I assumed there was "nothing much" to be found. I was to learn the opposite was true.

The project at Ark City, short for Arkansas City, investigated Wichita sites which were in the proposed construction path of the US 77 Bypass for Arkansas City and the U.S. 166 Highway Corridor upgrade. Waldo Wedel, of the Smithsonian Institution, had done preliminary work in the area in 1940, and his early work classifying artifact assemblages from the area, forms the basis for all subsequent research. The name Wedel applied to these sites, Great Bend aspect, "was used ... to describe a series of sites that share great similarities in material culture, economy, and settlement pattern" (Hoard, Robert J. editor. 2012 *Archeological Investigations Arkansas City, Kansas*. Kansas Historical Society Contract Archeological Publication 26, pg 30).

When I arrived in 1994, I was offered the position as field lab director. A field lab is responsible for the processing of all items from the sites including: ceramics, chipped and ground stone, bone (animal, bird, fish, and reptile), mollusks, plant and soil samples, charcoal, and other miscellaneous items. The artifacts were cleaned, stabilized (if necessary), packed and shipped to the main archeology lab at the KSHS in Topeka. There the artifacts were labeled, analyzed, and a report published.

The two projects cut through portions of eight Great Bend aspect sites with deep, bell-shaped pits, most of which produced an abundance of artifacts. Dates from C-14 samples ranged between 800 and 1800. "The excavations at these sites became the largest archeological investigation ever undertaken in Kansas. In the end, a total of over 600 subsurface pit features were excavated, along with numerous features of other types" (Hoard, Robert J. editor. 2012

Archeological Investigations Arkansas City, Kansas. Kansas Historical Society Contract Archeological Publication 26, pg 1).

No surface traces remained of the Wichita houses, which they constructed of poles and prairie grass. However, the bell-shaped cache, or storage, pits they used to securely stockpile extra food and personal items remained. When excavated, these sub-surface pits, which could be up to six feet deep, produced a wealth of artifacts and information for archeologist. The soil at Ark City is acidic but luckily, the Wichita dumped ash from their hearths, or fire pits, along with trash, into old pits they no longer used. This ash neutralized the acidic soil, thus preserving perishable items such as bone tools, delicate fish and bird bone, and even fish scales. I was amazed at the number of items the features produced! It is the largest collection of artifacts ever retrieved from such sites in Kansas. Some of the bone arrived in the lab looking like it had been buried yesterday—a dream for any archaeologist!

Along with artifacts removed during excavations, all the soil from the cache pits was bagged for water flotation. Each bag of feature fill (sediment) was processed to retrieve artifacts too small to see during excavation, plus minute plant and seed remains. These samples were also sent to the Topeka lab.

Individuals interested in detailed information about this intriguing project may contact the
Kansas State Historical Society, Topeka, Kansas.
The published report contains 537 pages with a
number of charts, diagrams and photographs of
features and artifacts. The report is also available
online.

Along with the vast experience and knowl-
edge I acquired working on the Ark City project,
I was privileged to form sev-
eral new friendships. Mr.
Virgil Swift, Jr., the cultural
resource manager for the
Wichita tribe, made a number
of trips to Ark City from his
home in Anadarko, Oklahoma,
throughout the project. Marlin
Hawley was the field director,
and my supervisor. Marlin, and
his assistant, Fred Scott, are
both very competent, experi-
enced archaeologist. I learned
a great deal from them and we
remain friends to this day.

Marlin F. Hawley
at site 14CO501,
Arkansas City,
Kansas, 1995.

The following pictures, including the bone
beads (page 12) and jar (page 33), are from the
Arkansas City, Kansas, project, courtesy of the
Archeology Office KSHS, Topeka, Kansas, and
Kansas Department of Transportation. Robert J.

Hoard, editor, 2012. *Archeological Investigations at Arkansas City, Kansas,* Contract Publication No. 26.

Included are the site locations. The archeological site code, or number, assigned by the Smithsonian Institute for Kansas, is the number 14. The next letters indicate the county, CO signifies Cowley County, and sites are recorded in numerical order in which they are recorded, starting with number one. For example, 14CO 385 indicates a site in the state of Kansas, in Cowley County, and the 385th site recorded.

14 CO385
Small rabbit effigy of hematite (iron oxide)
enlarged to show details, actual length 3/4"

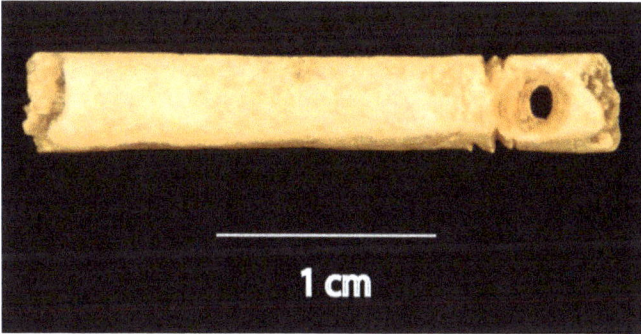

14C0331
Base of fragmentary bone needle

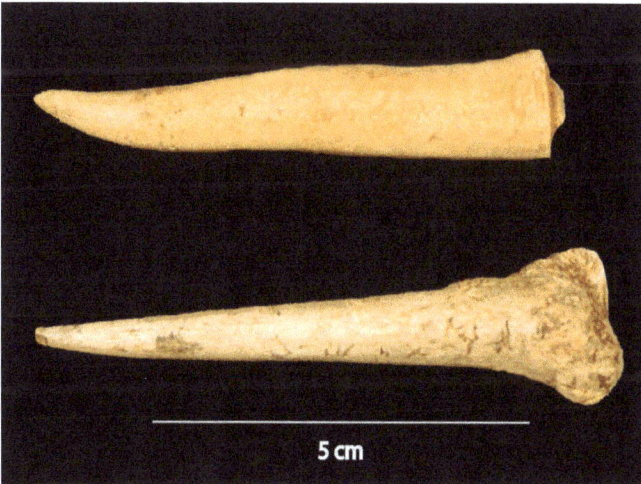

14C03
Two bone awls

14CO385 646-11	14CO1509 43-17	14CO382 126-2	14CO385 386-19	14CO385 687-12	14CO385 237-4	14CO382 106-1

14CO385 723-6	14CO385 646-14	14CO385 580-10	14CO385 599-21	14CO501 834-1	14CO1509 21-21	14CO382 176-1

14CO501 372-1	14CO501 108-1	14CO385 421-2	14CO1509 83-3	14CO385 580-7	14CO3 366-3	14CO385 559-14

14CO501 325-2	14CO501 359-1	14CO385 565-5	14CO501 271-1	14CO501 378-4	14CO331 152-17	14CO501 514-1

10 cm

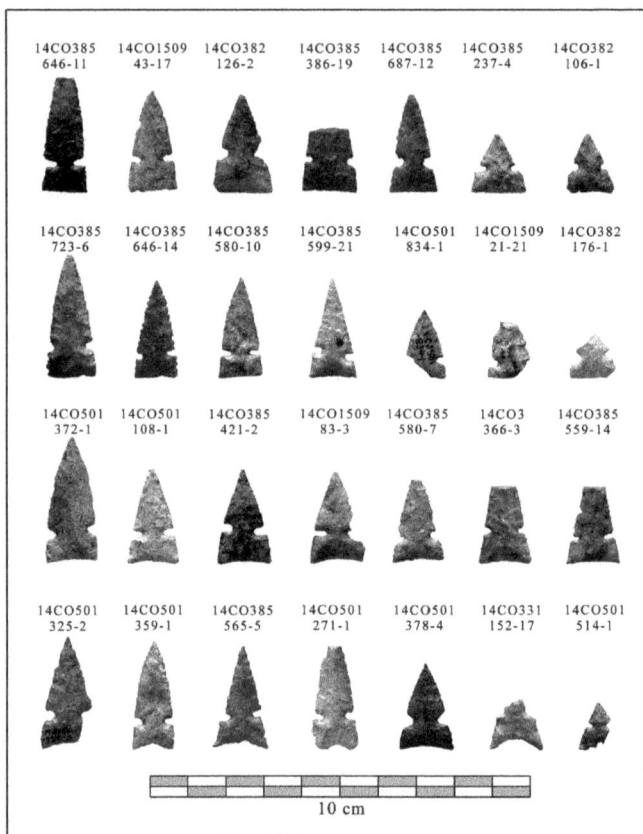

Washita projectile points

46

Cache pit at 14CO331
Partially excavated feature containing
bone concentration

For Further Reading

The literature on the Wichita-speaking peoples, especially as manifest in the archaeological record, is vast and growing, thanks to a renewed interest in the past 15 to 20 years. The standard archaeological treatment remains Waldo R. Wedel's 1959 volume, *An Introduction to Kansas Archeology*, published by the Bureau of American Ethnology, Smithsonian Institution. Although dated, Wedel's investigations of pre-contact Wichita sites in Kansas laid the foundation for all subsequent research. A short, modern, overview of research on the Great Bend aspect—the collective, archaeological manifestation of the Wichita peoples in Kansas—can be found in Donald J. Blakeslee and Marlin F. Hawley's chapter, "The Great Bend Aspect," published in *Kansas Archeology*, a book edited by Robert J. Hoard and William E. Banks and published by the University Press of Kansas in 2006. Hawley and Blakeslee also have published a wide-ranging, *An Annotated Bibliography of Great Bend-Wichita Archeology and Ethnohistory*, in the journal *The Kansas Anthropologist* in 2003. Again, while now somewhat dated, it includes references to articles and books on all aspects of Wichita history, ethnography, language, and archaeology. For those with a serious interest in the Wichita and the Great Bend aspect, this is still a good place to start.

Readers of this volume may want to consult George A. Dorsey's magnificent collection of Wichita mythology, first published by the Carnegie Institution in 1904, and fortunately reprinted by the University of Oklahoma Press. The volume is *The Mythology of the Wichita*. Dorsey's introduction includes many details about Wichita culture and life to the beginning of the twentieth century. A little known paper by archaeologists William T. Brogan and John D. Reynolds, entitled *Kansas Archeology Training Program: Experimental Archeology, Construction of a Grass Lodge*, is worth the effort to find. Published in the *Journal of the Kansas Anthropological Association*, this 1982 paper pulled together ethnographic, archaeological, and practical detail in building traditional, Wichita grass houses. One of the authors, the late John Reynolds, built the grass house that graces the Wichita exhibit in the Kansas Museum of History in Topeka.

More recent accounts of Wichita culture and history can be found in W.W. Newcomb's 1976 book, *The People Called Wichita*, published in the Indian Tribal Series out of Phoenix. Historian F. Todd Smith has also recounted a thorough history of the Wichita from 1540 into the latter nineteenth century in his book, *The Wichita Indians*, published in 2000 by Texas A&M Press. These volumes eschew detailed discussions of Wichita archaeology, but are still of great interest in following the Wichita into their contact with European societies, beginning in the mid-sixteenth century.

The list could go on and on. Not all of these works are readily available, but many are obtainable through interlibrary loan and some are available on the internet. Unfortunately, the internet is home to much unreliable information, so care and judgment must be taken in pursuit of information in that manner.

Other Books by
Susan A. Holland

Symbolism of Petroglyphs and Pictographs near Mountainair, New Mexico, the Gateway to Ancient Cities

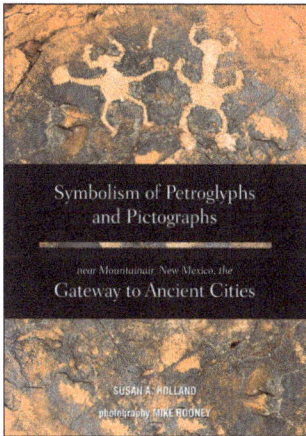

How a Boy Earned His Name

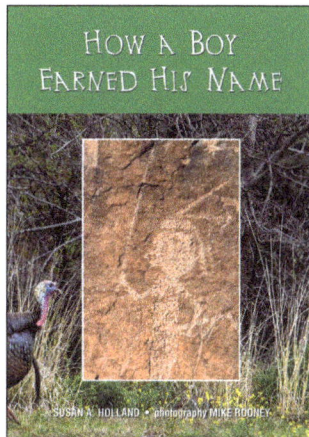

Available through Rowe Publishing, online bookstores, or ask for them at a local bookstore near you!

www.rowepub.com